Foreword
Chairman of t...

To see Heage windm... sight and for those of... in the 60s it is still a ... foresight of Derbyshire County Council back then the mill would have simply become a derelict tower as so many others have done. In April 1996 a steering group was formed and in July 1997 The Heage Windmill Society was formalised as a Charitable Trust.

The task was daunting, to restore to working order a mill that was 200 years old and that had not worked for some 90 years. The Friends of Heage Windmill were formed to organise fundraising and they, under the chair of Beverley Walters, threw themselves into the task of achieving, what at that time, was still a dream. The first Chairman of Heage Windmill Society was Councillor Mrs Margaret Kent who tirelessly worked to get the project off the ground. With assistance from Derbyshire County Council we eventually got the major funding in place. Not everything went to plan but after a frustrating period work finally started in July 2001.

Through the Friends and other local volunteers, shutters were made, old bearings removed and remade, stone walls built and the site generally made good, a huge effort by everyone. As Treasurer of the Trust I was pleased to be able to report that on completion of the work we had come in on budget.

Since opening to the public in June 2002 some 20,000 visitors have enjoyed visiting the mill. The work of managing and running the mill has to continue, our prime objective of preserving Heage Windmill for future generations has to be kept in mind and in 2005 when we had to replace two sails, from the original restoration, we got support from BBC Radio Derby and East Midlands Development Agency to complete this work.

Through the huge effort from the Friends and volunteers we are able to open the mill every weekend and have special openings for groups mid week. The continued enthusiasm from everyone ensures that visitors to Heage Windmill have a unique and memorable visit. The work of preserving Heage Windmill will give us new challenges in the future and I have to thank the people of Heage, Trustees, Friends and volunteers for their commitment to the mill.

A Short Introduction to Windmills

From the time, thousands of years ago, when man became a 'hunter/gatherer' he has had a requirement to crush various cereals to produce flour. Initially this was achieved by pounding the seeds in a mortar, or rubbing them between two stones.

Eventually the rotary hand quern evolved, using two stones, the top one of which rotated. This concept was then further developed by harnessing animals to rotate the upper stone and in the Roman era, about 40BC, the first water mills appeared, providing a constant

A typical post mill

source of power to the millstones. The first windmills to appear in England were in the 13th century and were the so called 'Post Mills', where a large wooden, boxlike structure containing the mill stones, was pivoted on top of a huge vertical post, such that the entire structure, including the sails, could be turned to face into the wind. Experience must have shown this to be essential since, if the wind got behind the sails, there was a grave danger that the mill would be blown over.

These were increasingly supplemented soon afterwards by the 'Tower Mills', which had a brick or stone cylindrical structure at the upper end of which there was a cap, carrying the sails, which could be turned into the wind, independently of the tower which supported it. The milling machinery was contained within the more durable structure, which also enjoyed more storage space than the post mills. The third form of mill was the 'Smock Mill' which in effect was a tower mill but was largely built of wood, and which was favoured in those parts of the country where timber was more freely available than stone or bricks. It has been estimated that in the early 19th century there were around 10,000 windmills in Britain.

During the 19th century the new milling techniques emerged, coupled with the availability of alternative power sources, such as steam and electricity, and together these spelt the end of the traditional wind and water mill as major commercial undertakings. A few, such as Heage windmill, have been restored to bring back to life technologies which were critical to our forebears.

Interested readers are guided to the bibliography in this book, if they would like to learn more about the evolution of the windmill.

The History of Heage Windmill - The Early Mill (1797-1850)

She (all windmills are called 'She') is the only stone tower mill with six sails in the British Isles. The first recorded reference to a windmill in Heage is an advertisement in the Derby Mercury of 16th June 1791:

"Heage windmill, to be erected - any mason inclined to undertake the stone building to attend at the mill, all materials laid down in place."

The stone appears to have been quarried almost on the site of the mill.

She was offered for letting as a new mill soon after, as recorded in the Derby Mercury 20th September 1798:

TO BE LET; And enter'd upon at Michaelmas next. A complete SMOCK WIND MILL with a fan tail, two pairs of Stones, and a good dressing Machine, every part is made in the most approv'd plans by Mr. Wass; stands in a good situation at Heage, in this county. – Also a neat House, Barn, &c. with 6 Acres of good Land adjoining the Mill, which may be enter'd upon at Lady-day next.

For particulars, apply to Mr. JAS. TURTON, Crich, who will let the same.

In 1803 an advert showed:

For Sale by Auction: Capital Smock wind mill contained a pair of Grey Stones, Black and French Ditto, with the Hulling Mill, Stable thereunder.

(A hulling mill was an adaptation used to prepare oatmeal).

Then in the Derby Mercury 7th February 1805:

SMOCK WIND CORN MILL and COPY-HOLD LAND, with possession at Lady-Day next. TO BE SOLD BY AUCTION by Mr. BARDWELL.

A Well-Erected and Substantial SMOCK WIND CORN MILL in good repair, and full employ, situated at Heage aforesaid, together with a convenient Messuage or Dwelling-house, Drying Kiln, Malt House,

Barn, Stable, and suitable Outbuildings and Conveniences. And 5 Acres of Copyhold Land be the same or less thereunto adjoining, now in the Occupation of Mr. R. Ashby.

The Tenant will shew the Premises; and for further Particulars apply to Mr. BARDWELL of Chesterfield.

In the Derby Mercury August 21st 1816:

TO BE LET,
WITH IMMEDIATE POSSESSION

A Capital good Smock WINDMILL with three pairs of Stones, and Dressing, Drying Kiln, &c. as also a neat good Dwelling House, with four Acres of Land attached thereto, situate at Heage, in the County of Derby.

For further Particulars and to treat for the same, apply to Mr. J. WALTERS, on the premises; or Mr. WHYSALL, Mare Hay, near Ripley.

Between 1805 and 1816 therefore, a grain drying kiln and some small outbuildings had been constructed next to the mill. The windmill operated with four common sails, until she was bought by the Shore family in 1850 (see later). A painting, owned by Paul Harrison from Worcestershire, shows her in this form.

This technically excellent painting, (artist unknown), which is thought to be dated about 1850, shows clearly that at that time there was no fantail fitted, only a simple boat shaped cap with a platform at the rear. The mill was probably being turned into the wind by an internal worm drive, operated by a chain from outside the mill. In the foreground adjacent to the mill is the kiln building, where the grain was dried before milling. Soon after 1850 the sails must have been changed to include two spring and two common sails, and a fantail fitted, as shown in the photo opposite, but we have no record of when this was actually done.

Heage windmill in about 1850
By courtesy of the
Mills Archive Trust

The Shore Family at Heage (1850-1919)

Arrival

Heage windmill, with four sails and a fantail, appears on the hill, whilst the water and steam mills owned by the Shores are in the valley below (c 1870).

Up to the present time it has been thought that, based on a reference dated 1846, Isaac and John Shore may have moved to the village in 1818 from Norton Hall, near Sheffield. Recent studies have suggested however that there were 'Shores' living in Heage in 1785, when a John Shore married Hannah, in Duffield. They had four sons and certainly by 1850 members of the family, are reported to have purchased the windmill, trading as millers and grocers. We have noted incidentally, at various times, the family name seems to have been spelt 'Shaw'. All this is an area of continued investigation.

The Shores in Business

Below the windmill in Nether Heage, stood an old water mill fed by a meagre stream that flowed across the road forming a ford. The mill stood by the roadside and as a result had reasonably easy access. Its only problem was that shortage of water in the summer prevented the mill operating. The Shores saw the potential of this mill and purchased it, fitting an auxiliary slack-fired (poor quality coal) steam boiler and a steam engine in order that milling could continue when there was neither wind nor water available. By 1900 Kelly's directory identifies the brothers as being coal owners. Their coal mine may have been on the edge of the coal seams that occurred on the hillside at Nether Heage, and which could well have been worked as open footrills (or adits).

Heage is believed to have the only group of mills in the country where a windmill, a watermill and a steam mill were all owned by the same company. The mill has been referred to as 'Ned's mill'. Ned may have been a millwright involved in major work at the mill in 1850, possibly fitting new machinery. However in 1857 Edward Gell was 'manager - corn miller' so it is possible that this was 'Ned'.

'Trouble at t' Mill'

The previous photograph, dated about 1870, appears to show the mill with two common and two spring sails, a black boat shaped cap and a fantail with 14 slim blades. At some time after this 4 patent sails were evidently fitted, since in February 1894 when the mill was tailwinded (a severe gust of wind blew from behind the mill) in one of the worst February gales in living memory, the windshaft broke in two, wrecking the cap and the sails of the mill.

A contemporary photograph (probably taken by the Fritchley Quaker, Mr Hill) shows the miller and his son standing in the wreckage. Amidst the wreckage the striking rod for the patent sails can be seen, as can the shutters.

The boy can be seen at the far left.

Fortunately, the steam and water mill in the valley was able to cope with the remaining winter demands, but it was necessary to repair the windmill to fully cope with demand. No doubt, the free source of power was also a consideration. After the tail winding in 1894 the mill was soon reconstructed, and the opportunity taken to further modernise the

An early image of the windmill with six sails and complete with an ogee cap

sails and top equipment.

A new cast iron windshaft with a six arm cross was supplied by the Butterley Company of Ripley and fitted by the local millwright George Chell of Fritchley. Chell was assisted by a local carpenter, Joseph Spendlove of Heage, who made the new ogee (onion-shaped) cap, crowned with a ball finial. The six sails were of the 'patent' type with automatic striking gear linked by a central 'spider' and striking rod through the centre of the windshaft, and operated remotely via a projecting lever at the rear of the cap fitted with a chain down to ground level. The present shot curb was probably installed at this time, using a relatively sophisticated roller race and a double pinion fantail drive mechanism.

Better Times Then Decline (1894-1919)

The mills must have prospered as at one time the Shore brothers had seven waggoners delivering corn and hauling flour. These were based at Heage Hall and were employed to pick up corn for grinding from an area covering eight to ten miles. This would be in addition to farmers who delivered, and collected their own flour. Local farmers turned more and more land back to pasture and other crops, reducing the amount of corn available locally for milling and finally the start of World War I accelerated the downfall of many English windmills.

The mill in decline c.1914
Note the tiles missing from the kiln.

A photo dating about the time of the First World War shows the mill and sails complete, but damage to the kiln roof is visible. This may represent the start of the decline of the windmill and its outbuildings.

The windmill and the miller's cottage in the 1940s

The mill, under the control of Mr T J (Tom) Shore, who was the eldest son of Joseph and grandson of the founder, continued in production until 1916. From then she only worked spasmodically, until in 1919, she was once again damaged in a severe gale, this time losing most of the blades in the fantail.

The development of new roller milling systems, the demand for white flour, the concentration of the milling industry near to ports with the huge imports of grain from Canada and North America and the increase in motorised transport, made it uneconomical to repair the mill and continue milling at Heage.

The condition of the mill steadily declined and photographs taken in the 1930s show the mill had become quite derelict. Abandoned and sadly neglected, she was put up for sale in 1934, when Henry Smith Allsop, who lived in the miller's house below the mill, bought her, together with a small plot of surrounding land, at auction for just £25. Some of the essential cast iron parts of the machinery were removed, possibly during the Second World War scrap drive.

Rex Wailes, the most famous of the early mill enthusiasts, visited the mill in 1961, and with Paul Baker describes his findings in the 1961-62 Transactions of the Newcomen Society volume XXXIV:

'There is a shot curb, with 24 rollers and six truck wheels; the rollers were held in the ring by special cast-iron carriers and ran in a cast-iron angled inner flange bolted to the curb.

The winding gear comprised a single pair of bevels each driving a spur pinion in the tail of the cap and between the sheers. A worm wheel on the horizontal spindle was driven by a hand-operated worm.

Heage windmill had the smallest number of cogs (teeth) on the brake wheel of any in Derbyshire, Leicestershire and Nottinghamshire at 60 wooden cogs with a 4¾ inch pitch. They meshed with 45 iron cogs on the wallower.

50 cast-iron teeth, cast in sections and bolted on to the great spur wheel, replaced 70 cogs of 3 inch pitch in two staggered rows.'

Part of cap hand winding mechanism

Note: The two staggered rows of cogs on the great spur wheel would have required two rows of cogs on the stone nuts. This system was part of the development of gearing in an attempt to provide a smoother drive but which appears to have been unsuccessful.

The use of a double pinion drive in a windmill, as mentioned earlier, is very unusual and the system was drawn for Rex Wailes and Paul Baker by Kenneth Charles Lord, and was reproduced in the Transaction of the Newcomen Society in 1962.

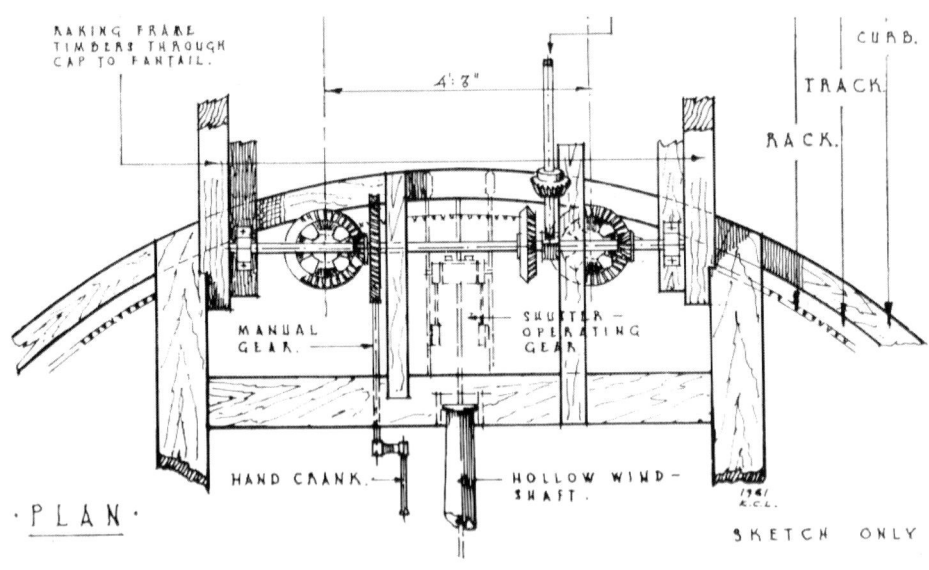

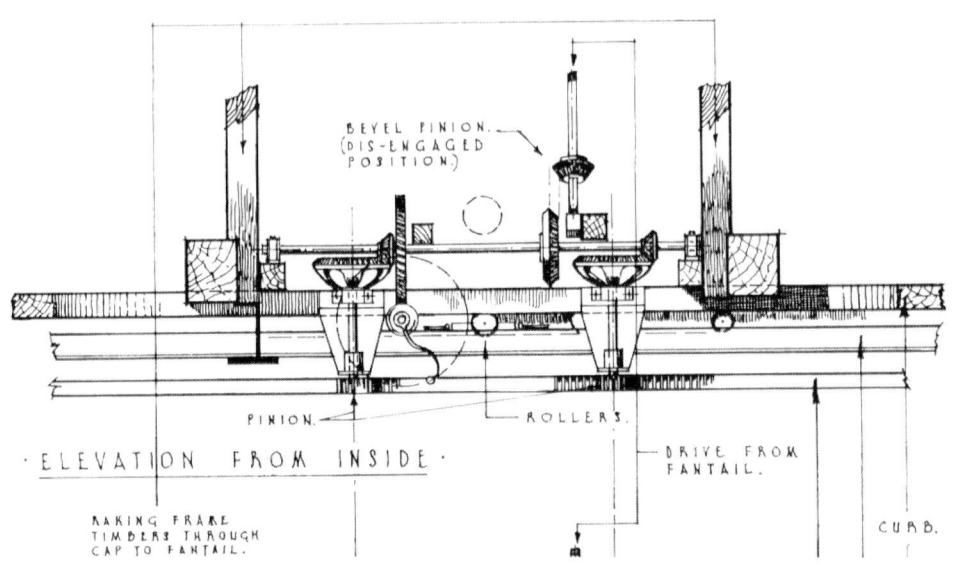

Plan and Elevation drawings of the mill winding gear
(reproduced by courtesy of the Newcomen Society)

The First Restoration Programme

A photograph taken in 1955 shows the mill, with only the remains of the sails in place but otherwise, more or less intact. She was struck by lightning in 1961 and a photograph taken in 1967 shows only the remnants of the sails and a stub where the fantail and its staging had been.

She was first listed as a building of special historic interest, Grade II, in September 1961. Prompted by a proposal to convert the mill to a house a Building Preservation Order (the first ever in the county under the 1962 Town & Country Planning Act) was placed on the mill in May 1966.

Following this the mill was listed Grade II* on 27th May 1966. A photo in 1967 shows the mill, shortly before Derbyshire County Council purchased her from the owner Mrs J. Wilders for £350 in 1968, with the sails almost bare and most of the ribs of the cap are showing. Trees were now growing about the mill, which would have spoilt the airflow to drive the mill had it been in operation.

The mill in 1955, still in a reasonable condition

The Windmill in 1967

During the early 1970s restoration work was carried out on behalf of Derbyshire County Council by the millwrights R. Thompson and Son, of Alford in Lincolnshire, when new floors, sails, cap covering and skeleton fantail were fitted, and certain parts, including the millstones, reinstated.

The sails were hoisted into place on 15th March 1972 and the fantail was lifted into place three days later. This work cost £7245.07. The repairs gave a much better external appearance to the mill although the use of aluminium for the cap was far from traditional and did not stand the test of time, partly because the copper nails used were not suitable. The work programme restored some internal machinery but did not permit the cap to rotate, so the mill was unable to operate.

The windmill and cottage during 1970s restoration work; the fantail is not yet in place.

Despite the restoration the County Council made little attempt to open her to the public and it was not until 1989, when the Midland Mills Group first provided the guides, that an Open Day was held and more than 500 visitors were received.

The mill house was purchased by Mr Bill Henshaw (deceased) about 1987, and with only limited openings of the windmill, it was a quiet, secluded location for most of the time.

In the following years very little more was done to the mill, and it became clear that further maintenance was becoming urgent. With increasing financial restrictions placed upon them, the County Council was unable to invest sufficient further resources to adequately maintain and develop the mill, and its condition commenced to deteriorate.

In 1993 the sails broke free in high winds, despite having no shutters, and this resulted in the smashing of parts of the brakewheel. Fortunately the County Council soon had this repaired by the millwrights R H Thompson and Son from Lincolnshire. The mill was once again struck

Soon after the first restoration in 1970. Note the absence of shutters and blades in the fan tail.

by lightning in July 1995, destroying one sail, damaging some floor beams and causing some minor internal damage. After this a lightning conductor was fitted and two sails replaced. Some other heavy timbers and the sheers in the cap were replaced in 1998, again by R H Thompson and Son.

The Midland Mills Group and Derbyshire County Council

The Midland Mills Group was initially approached by Derbyshire County Council Rangers in about 1987 to act as guides on the occasions when the mill was planned to be annually opened to the public. The first such opening was in 1989. As a result of this close contact and recognising the importance of this mill, the Midland Wind and Water Mills Group (MMG) took the initiative of liaising with Derbyshire County Council and arranging more public openings, together with organising volunteer working parties to tidy up the surrounds, clean up the mill and limit further deterioration. The work immediately created a 'cared-for' feeling within the mill, and the de-rusting of much of the ironwork and painting it black was particularly effective. Unfortunately, following the lightning damage in 1995 the County Council felt obliged to deny access to the mill to anyone on safety grounds, and the work was halted, leaving some of the ironwork still in its priming paint colour.

Volunteers clearing the site in 1995; the end wall of the old kiln can be seen on the left and the condition of the site is obvious.

Heage Windmill Society and the Friends

The working parties had generated considerable local interest and the Heage Windmill Society (HWS) was established in 1996, becoming formally established as a Charitable Trust (No.1065980) on 1st July 1997, with the aims of restoring the mill, providing a visitor centre, a new access and a small car park. It was the aim of the Society to commence the restoration work in the mill's bicentenary year, 1997 and about this time an active support group, 'The Friends of Heage Windmill', was formed.

Heage Windmill Society and Derbyshire County Council joined forces to make applications to various organisations seeking financial help in restoring the windmill to an operational state, including the necessary visitor centre and the provision of a new access road and car park.

The original track to the mill was too steep and narrow for present day requirements, and the Highway Authority was against additional access from the steep Dungeley Hill. A new, almost level, route was therefore proposed across open fields from the Chesterfield Road. Provisional agreement had previously been reached with the local farmer for the line of the new road.

Further Restoration – Back to Working Order

In 1998 the owners of the mill, Derbyshire County Council, spent £36,000 from their planned maintenance budget on emergency repairs, replacing rotten timbers beneath the cap (the sheers) and two of the sails. They also installed the much needed lightning conductors.

In the summer of the same year, Heage Windmill Society was granted £38,000 from English Heritage to restore the masonry of the tower. The biggest grant came in September 1998 when the National Heritage Lottery Fund awarded £163,855. Waste Recycling Environmental Ltd. (WREN) gave a grant of £80,000 towards a visitor centre and the access road and Amber Valley Borough Council granted another £20,000 for general improvements.

However, before the work on the windmill could begin, the new access road had to be constructed. The negotiations by Derbyshire County Council for the line of the road and the right of way were long and complicated, delaying the start of the project for almost two years. Finally agreement was reached for an access road across the fields from Chesterfield Road to a car park adjacent to the mill. All was set for the work to be completed and the windmill to be working and open to visitors for spring 2001.

In August 2000 the work on the road began and ceased almost immediately. The further legal difficulties which caused this delay took time to solve and when activities were able to recommence the contractor had work elsewhere. Progress was then further delayed by the fuel crisis followed by a winter with the heaviest rain on record, making the ground too waterlogged to work on.

Eventually, at the beginning of March the ground was dry enough for work to resume but, unfortunately, this coincided with an outbreak of foot and mouth disease. The Windmill Society perhaps became yet another victim of the disease and also became very frustrated since for many months they just could not proceed with this exciting project.

The enforced delays to the project resulted in additional costs, largely due to the escalation in contractors' prices, in excess of £25,000, due to the time delays experienced. A further additional cost was identified when the electricity supply company reported that the supply cable on Dungeley Hill had insufficient capacity to meet the needs of the mill. This resulted in the supply having to be brought from Chesterfield Road, about a quarter of a mile away, and a large transformer was installed close to the mill.

The opportunity was however taken of having all services ducted in the same trench, which saved some money, but even so an additional £22,000 was required. WREN was again approached and fortunately provided the funds needed for this work.

The requirement for specialist plaster (it's lime based) for the mill's interior walls was not foreseen at the time of the original application for funding, and this caused another problem, but an additional special grant of £27,000 from English Heritage helped to resolve the problem. The Society itself made a significant contribution as 'match funding' by way of volunteer labour in carrying out work at the mill and her surroundings, by local fund raising events and obtaining support from the local community.

By running various fund raising events including 'Sponsor a Shutter/Fantail Blade/Square Foot of Stone Floor' schemes the Society raised over £10,000 towards the restoration costs. Volunteers from the Friends made significant practical contributions including making all the 126 shutters, the new rollers for the cap and the millstone governor to control the quality of the flour. The volunteer team has also repaired or rebuilt much of the dry stone walling around the mill. In addition they carried out landscaping to the mill surroundings and access way. The total cost of the project was about £420,000. and included the production of specially designed display panels, provided for interpretive purposes.

Aerial view showing end of new access road and car park; the sails are facing South West.

The work was finally completed and the mill was formally opened by local TV presenter Kathy Rochford in May 2002 and the mill came back into life again, after eighty years of being idle, adding what has proved to be an outstanding feature to local tourism and enhancing the environment. In 2003 the restored windmill produced her first batch of flour for many years, and continues to mill when flour is required and the wind allows, providing flour for sale at the windmill and at local farmers markets.

Guides ready for action

The mill is open regularly at weekends from April to the end of October and on Bank Holidays. Arrangements are available for schools and other parties of visitors to be guided round the mill on days other than normal open days. The guides usually adopt the costume associated with the mill about 1900, when she was in commercial use.

Some of the Work Undertaken Since the 2002 Restoration

Keeping a windmill going is like painting the Forth Bridge - you are always at it! Since the mill opened in May 2002 (five years ago at the time of writing) a number of projects have been completed to either improve the mill or simply to keep her running. Some diverse examples are listed below:-

Two New Sails Fitted

During the autumn of 2004 some ominous signs of rot were spotted on a couple of the whips (main spars) and a decision was taken, for safety reasons, to remove them. The whips, which were not replaced during the 2002 restoration programme, are believed to be from a set of three which were fitted in about 1995, although no accurate records had been retained.

A major fund raising initiative was set up to fund the work (estimated to cost £6,000 each, excluding the shutters, which were almost new and so were reused from the previous sails) and new sails, made from laminated Siberian larch, were ordered from the millwright Neil Medcalf of Boston. Getting these huge pieces of timber is not an instant matter and the mill ran through 2005 with only four sails – something mills with six sails can do in an emergency.

Removing leading boards for winter

The new ones were made off site and were finally put in place just one day before the opening day for the 2006 season.

In view of the long procurement time scale involved a spare whip has been bought and is being carefully stored against the day the third sail begins to show those ugly tell tale signs.

And An Improvement To All The Sails

Despite the national rush to use the wind to generate electricity, at Heage we have found that the wind speed was often too low to even permit the mill to idle. In order to improve this an addition has been made to each sail known as *'Leading Boards'*. These consist of pieces of wood, about 225mm wide and 25mm thick which run the full length of the front edge of the sail, aimed at increasing the sail area by about 20% and, so far, our hopes have been realised. The mill is now able to turn freely in quite a light breeze. The design is such that about 50% of the new board area can be un-bolted and stored through the winter months when the mill is normally silent, and winter winds blow.

Funding came from a variety of sources but we are extremely grateful to Radio Derby's Money Mountain and to the East Midlands Development Agency for making significant grants to help in financing the work on the sails.

Dampness In The Mill

The mill was quite damp when the Trust took it over and it was some time before the probable cause was established as being water permeating through the soft ironstone rock from which the tower was built. The ventilation in the mill was found to be poor and new, hopper type windows have been fitted to the upper floors whilst an improved rear hatch has been built into the cap which allowed moisture to escape and at the same time gave much better access to the fantail staging. As an additional safeguard a circular gutter, attached to cap, was fabricated from aluminium with drain spouts throwing water clear at the rear of the mill, just below the cap stage. All signs to date are that we have significantly reduced the effects of moisture ingress whilst not changing the visual effect of the mill.

New Flour Dresser

When flour was again first produced in 2003 we were only able to mill the wholemeal variety. We knew that in the past the mill had had a dresser installed which separated the meal into various grades of flour so we decided to have one made and installed on the meal (ground) floor. It was necessary to research the construction of dressers and eventually an acceptable design was reached.

(cf picture and explanation on page 31)

The rotary wire drum flour dresser was designed by HWS and a local craftsman, Gordon Cooper, was instructed to carry out the work. The new machine was duly installed. After some teething problems Heage windmill is now able to grade meal, as required, and even to produce white flour.

Flour Storage and Processing

Scales for weighing flour

Storage cupboards on Meal (Ground) Floor

Flour has been produced since 2003 and when the meal emerges from between the mill stones a chain of subsequent events has to be followed to ensure the product will meet necessary hygiene standards. The flour must be stored in a manner such as to prevent rodent action and the flour must be weighed and packaged in a secure manner. To facilitate these measures a large, metal-backed, but fully ventilated, wooden cupboard has been built, again by a local craftsman, Clive Bates, for storage of the product. He has also constructed a stout wooden bench on which the packaging operations are conducted. These components have been designed and built in traditional styles and have quickly blended into the work area.

Access Road Maintenance

Brian Boucher gets his 1922 Aveling and Porter roller ready.

The 'type 1' gravel (magnesian limestone from Bolsover quarry) surface of the road, in the five years since it was constructed, had become severely pot holed. The son of one of the Trustees, Brian Boucher, just happened to own a working 1922 Aveling and Porter steam roller and was willing to bring it to the site under its own steam. During a busy weekend the pot holes were cut out, loose filling inserted and then the roller did what it knows best – compacted the material, and once again we have a sound roadway.

*The mill was built to Imperial Dimensions
and these have been used primarily in the following text.*

Machinery Of The Mill

A very basic description of the structure and mechanism of the mill is set out in this section. For more information on windmills in general please consult one of the books listed in the bibliography.

The fundamental purpose of a windmill is to extract power from the wind and convert it into useful energy to drive the corn grinding stones and other equipment, and for this the windmill contains a train of drive and control machinery. The following parts of the mill fulfil this essential function (the reference numbers given before each part name refer to the key numbers in the sectional drawing on page 22).

1   Tower

The mill tower is the basic structure, which gives rise to the name for the type of mill. It is solidly constructed of local sandstone and forms a truncated cone, 22ft 11in (7m) diameter at the base and tapering inwards towards the top. The tower is about 26ft 3in (8m) high, surmounted by the cap, adding a further 13ft 2in (4m), producing a total height of 39ft 5in (12m).

The cap is lowered back in place on the tower. The six arm cross is clearly visible.

Structurally it provides a very strong shape to resist the horizontal forces from the wind, and the circular shape enables the cap to swing round so that the sails face the wind from any direction.

There are two doorways and beside the east door is an inscription WSM 1850, the significance of which is not clear. There is also a chimney and fireplace built into the stonework of the tower.

2   Floors

The mill tower contains four internal floors of massive timber construction and a basement. The floors are known by their function: the entrance is on the meal floor, and the next up is the stone floor where the millstones are sited.

Above this is the bin floor, where grain awaiting milling is stored in bins, and finally at the top is the dust floor, which protects the 'clean' floors of the mill from the grease and dust dropping from the machinery in the cap.

3   Sails

The sails are the dominant feature of a windmill, and convert the force of the wind into rotational energy. In effect propeller blades, they present a large almost flat area slightly angled to the direction of the wind, and are mounted on the end of a projecting shaft near the top of the mill which enables them to rotate anticlockwise when the wind blows. This rotation provides the torque necessary to drive the machinery.

There are six sails, each 30ft (9m) long, at Heage windmill, which are 'patent' shuttered sails*. The sails fitted between 1972 and 2002 were in fact only the sail frames, and required the installation of 126 shutters i.e. 21 per sail, before they could function.

The hired crane dropping the last sail into place in 2002

The mill is rather unusual in having six sails; only three working six sailer mills now remain in the UK, and by far the majority of remaining windmills have four sails only. It is the only working six sailed mill built in stone.

*'Patent' sails are so called because
the design was patented by Sir William Cubitt in 1807.

Key To Heage Windmill And Its Machinery

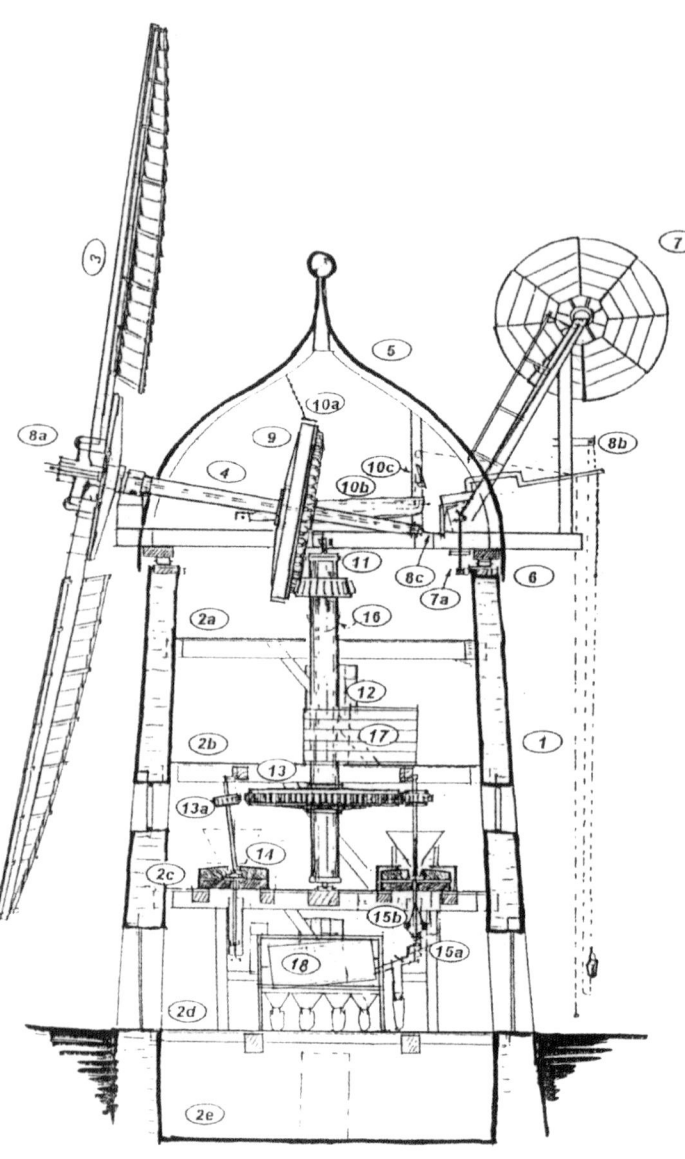

Section through Heage Windmill

Drawing Courtesy of Boucher & Sons.

1 Tower

2 Floors
 a) Dust Floor
 b) Bin Floor
 c) Stone Floor
 d) Ground Floor
 e) Basement

3 Sails

4 Windshaft

5 Cap

6 Curb

7 Fantail

8 Striking Gear
 a) Spider
 b) Striking Lever
 c) Striking Rod

9 Brakewheel

10 Brake
 a) Brake Band
 b) Brake Beam
 c) Striking Arm

11 Wallower

12 Upright Shaft

13 Great Spur Wheel
 a) Stone Nuts

14 Millstones

15 Tentering Gear
 a) Bridge Trees
 b) Governor

16 Sack Hoist

17 Grain Bin

18 Flour Sifting M/c

The old, aluminium covered cap removed for renovation. Note the iron cross on the right and skeleton fan tail on the left

4   Windshaft

The sails are supported on the rotating shaft or axle known as the 'windshaft', which takes the drive through to the inside of the mill. Supported in two large bearings at the neck and tail, and resting on heavy timbers that form the frame for the 'cap' of the mill, it is inclined at 12° to the horizontal. It is made of cast iron, and was made by the Butterley Company in 1894 after the previous windshaft broke in two when the mill became 'tail winded' in the 1894 gale.

Six arm iron cross during restoration

At the front end a six arm cross is keyed onto the windshaft on which the sails are fastened. The windshaft has a hollow core to permit the 'striking rod' to be passed through to facilitate the automatic adjustment of the shutters.

5   Cap

This is the roof of the mill, and comprises a substantial timber framework supporting the windshaft, brakewheel and other internal equipment. It was latterly roofed with aluminium sheeting on timber ribs, but old photographs show that it was previously boarded. Externally the cap has a large, 20ft 2in (6m), diameter ogee shape, following the traditional design of Derbyshire tower mills. The whole of the cap rotates to face the wind to enable the sails to work most effectively. During the 2001 programme the aluminium covering was replaced with two layers of larch boarding, interfaced with an impermeable membrane and covered by heavy duty canvas, painted white.

6   Curb

The top of the tower wall is finished off with two thick layers of oak timber on which is mounted a cast iron section known as the curb track. This is placed so that it is concentric with the wallower and set to level with a high degree of accuracy in order to form a smooth foundation upon which the cap can rotate.

The new curb, rack and two of the 24 rollers

The type of curb at Heage is known as a 'shot curb' because of its special construction incorporating a roller race (24 rollers) all round between the curb and the cap to reduce friction when the cap turns. This is quite rare in Britain, the normal arrangement being for the cap to slide on fixed greased plates, or occasionally on small castor wheels fixed to the cap beneath the principal load points.

The cap is maintained centrally by six truck (or steady) wheels running on the inside face of the curb.

7   Fantail

This is a mechanical device which automatically turns the cap into the wind. It is in effect a small subsidiary windmill having 8 blades mounted on the rear of the cap. The fantail turns when the wind strikes it obliquely and drives the cap round through a very low-geared rack and pinion mechanism.

Final adjustments to the fantail before the refurbished cap is lifted back onto the tower

The details of the drive at Heage are particularly interesting as it employs a double train of gearing with two pinions meshing with the rack. It is thought that no other drives of this pattern survive. If the wind is not strong enough to turn the fantail, there is provision made to turn the cap by hand. The winding handle requires about 3,000 turns for one complete rotation of the cap.

8   Striking gear

The striking gear is the mechanism for controlling the adjustment of the shutters in the sails, and hence starting and stopping the mill. It automatically controls it to some extent during changes in wind speed.

The opening and closing of each shutter in each sail is controlled by a sliding rod on the front of the sail, which is in turn connected to a mechanism at the centre known as the 'spider'.

The spider is connected by the striking rod passing through the hollow centre of the windshaft, which is connected to a long arm known as the 'striking lever' that projects out of the rear of the mill. A chain from ground level operates this lever and moves the striking rod in and out, to open or close the shutters.

Detail of the striking gear

The chain can be set to hold the shutters open (not working), or closed, or weighted in such a way that as the wind strength increases, the shutters will open to try to maintain the rotational speed of the sails.

9   Brakewheel

This is a large wooden wheel mounted on the windshaft within the cap of the mill, constructed in timber. It has a dual function: a) to provide the path for a brake and b) to provide the drive to the machinery through bevelled teeth or 'cogs' positioned on the rear face of the brakewheel which drive a bevelled gear wheel or 'wallower' fitted at the top of the main upright drive shaft.

The brakewheel is of timber clasp arm construction and originally had 60 wooden cogs, but at a later date these were cut off and replaced by cast iron toothed segments bolted on to its face. The eight new segments have a total of 100 teeth. The wooden brakewheel, complete with bolt-on iron teeth, is mounted on the iron windshaft.

The wooden brakewheel, complete with bolt-on iron teeth, is mounted on the iron windshaft.

10   Brake

A metal contracting band around the perimeter of the brakewheel forms the brake. The band is operated by a rope and lever mechanism from outside the back of the mill at ground level. The lever or 'brake beam' is of heavy timber (cf p.42) and this holds the brake on by its own weight; the brake is released by pulling on the rope to lift the beam up into a 'swinging catch'. The brake is normally used only for parking the mill, and is not a means of controlling speed or stopping the mill.

Detail of the brakewheel and the iron brake band

11   Wallower

The wallower is the name given to the bevel gear that takes the drive from the brakewheel to the upright shaft. It is of cast iron construction with a diameter of roughly 2½ft (760mm) and has 45 teeth.

12 Upright Shaft

Looking down on the wallower gear, inside its safety guard, at the upper end of the upright shaft, meshing with the brakewheel on the right.

This is the main vertical drive shaft down to the millstones at the bottom of the mill. It comprises a large section timber shaft, 17in (432mm) diameter, supported in a thrust or 'pot' bearing resting on a cross beam at stone floor level, and held by a vertical sleeve bearing at its top end.

A cast iron wallower is fitted at the top to engage with the cogs on the brakewheel. Power is passed from the wallower driven from the brakewheel down to a large gear wheel known as the 'great spur wheel' fixed lower down, above the level of the millstones.

The lower bearing of the wooden upright shaft. Note the iron reinforcing bands.

13 Great Spur Wheel

This is the large gear wheel transferring the drive to the two small pinions or 'stone nuts' driving the millstones. It is probable that other nuts were originally fitted to drive other machinery. It is constructed in timber, and originally had, very unusually, two rows of 70 wooden cogs with a pitch of 4¾ in (121mm), staggered by half a pitch. These appear to have been at some time cut off and replaced by cast iron segments having 50 teeth.

The decision was therefore made to restore the gearing in the condition they last operated.

The new teeth are in cast iron and are bolted on in sections. The stone nut, which transmits the drive to millstones, has a cast iron core, but the teeth are made of oily apple wood. This probably gives a 'fail safe' protection, since if the machinery jammed for any reason, the teeth would sheer off and are easily replaced.

The great spur wheel, clasp arm constructed, is mounted on the upright shaft.

Additionally however, before accurate machine cut gears became available, cast iron gears were very noisy and difficult to fit well. Wooden teeth or cogs on one side reduced the noise and, if necessary, could easily be pared down to improve the mesh.

14 The Millstones

Millstones are used in matched pairs for grinding grain into flour or animal feed. The upper stone of each pair rotates and is known as the runner stone. The lower stone is fixed and is known as the bed stone.

In order to meet varying milling requirements, the first pair (at the top of the stairs) has each been made in a single piece from Derbyshire millstone grit (known as Peak stones) which could be used for general purpose grinding, such as animal feeds etc., while the second pair has been built up from segments of a very

The cast iron stone nut, fitted with cogs made of apple wood

hard stone imported from France (known as French stones or French Burrs), which would normally be used for grinding hard wheat to make flour for bread. For each set of millstones, the drive to the runner stone is taken from a stone nut running on the great spur wheel.

The grooves in the stones are 'sharpened' from time to time by a hand-chipping process (cf p.34). Only the French Stones are presently operational at Heage. Both sets are about 4ft 6in(1.4m) diameter and rotate at up to about 120 r.p.m.

One of the pairs of millstones, contained in the wooden vat or tun. The 'furniture' above includes the hopper which holds the corn.

The bridge tree carries the governor*, mounted on the stone spindle. The meal spout enters the dresser on the left. *Made by Derek Walker.

15   Tentering gear   (cf picture on previous page)

Each pair of stones requires a bridging tree to support the runner stone and a set of tentering gear to enable the gap between the stones to be adjusted and set to give the correct fineness of grinding. This is manually adjusted, but in addition it is desirable in a windmill to have a governor providing further automatic adjustment to compensate for the varying speed of the wind or the load on the mill.

16   Sack hoist

Every mill is fitted with at least one sack hoist to lift sacks of grain up through a series of trap doors to the bin floor at the top of the mill where it can be emptied into the bins or hoppers (17) to commence its descent by gravity through the milling process.

The sack hoist mechanism is located in the top of the mill just below the wallower, from which it derives its motion by a friction mechanism. It is operated by a cord, which passes through all the floors and when pulled from below, this lifts the friction drive wheel to contact the rotating underside of the wallower, thus driving the hoist.

Auxiliary machinery

Most mills had some auxiliary machinery of various types, but none of the originals has survived at Heage. Examples might include a machine for cleaning or dressing the grain before milling, and various types of flour machine for sieving and grading the meal after grinding, or even elevators to raise the meal for further processing at a higher level.

The sack hoist is driven by friction from the underside of the wallower and lifts the heavy sacks of corn to the top of the mill. The pulley is raised to activate the hoist, and is operated from below.

There is a reference to a 'good dressing machine' being in place when the mill was new, but it is not known what other machinery was subsequently incorporated. In order to be able to grade the meal which emerges from the stones, and to enable white flour to be produced, a rotary wire dressing machine has been designed and is installed on the ground floor. Since the original drive connection to the great spur wheel has been lost the new machine is powered by electricity.

The dresser has three sizes of wire mesh on the inclined rotating drum, the meal entering at the high end of the drum and then falling onto the finest mesh. This allows the fine white flour to pass through and into the first sack.

The meal then passes to the next coarser mesh, where the fine bran and coarse flour pass through into the second sack to produce 'middlings' which is a coarse brown flour.

The final mesh is the coarsest and the majority of the bran falls through this into the third sack. Any large particles in the meal,

A view of the side of the wire dressing machine used to grade the meal and produce white flour

e.g. grains of wheat, pass over all the mesh sieves and fall over the end of the drum to be collected in the fourth sack.

Drying the Grain: The Kiln

There has been a kiln at Heage for 200 years, since an advertisement in The Derby Mercury (5th August 1802) offers the mill to let, *'with drying kiln, cowshed and gardens'*. The kiln had not figured in earlier advertisements so it was probably newly built. When corn or oats were harvested, in this variable climate of ours, they were often too damp to be successfully processed. Whilst only hand querns had been used this did not matter too much since small batches of grain could be taken from storage and dried as required. The increased use of water and wind power meant that larger batches of dried cereals were need at one time so drying kilns were introduced, using wood, peat or coal as fuel, aimed at reducing the moisture content to about 12-18%.

In the north of Britain, certainly above about Northamptonshire, drying kilns were a common feature at both wind and water mills. They were sometimes built integrally with water mills e.g. at nearby Stainsby Water Mill, but often were free-standing buildings.

The kiln at Heage had one upper drying floor and was about 24ft (7.3m) long, 15ft (4.6m) wide. The only old photos we have show it with a corrugated iron roof. When built however it would have had a roof of stone slabs, some of which were lifted slightly so that smoke could escape, or perhaps at a later date, with a louvered vent in the ridge.
(See on page 4 the earlier Painting of Heage Windmill, as a four sail mill; the kiln is in front of the mill.)

Model of a typical Derbyshire kiln used for drying grain

At the centre of one end of the ground floor of the building was the hearth or fireplace. From this was built a vaulted structure of brick, which extended to the walls at the drying floor level, providing a 'funnel', the sides of which could be entered to tend the fire and where fuel could be stored. The actual drying area, across the 'funnel' was probably about 12ft (3.7m) square, with iron 'T' bars running across in one direction, about 12 inches apart. Onto these bars 12in (305mm) square perforated ceramic tiles were placed, providing a complete flat surface upon which the grain could be placed.

The grain was brought into the building at drying floor level and was spread to form an even layer 2-3in (53-76mm) thick. The fire was lit and heat (plus smoke) floated up through the holes in the tiles and drying commenced. The grain was turned frequently with a wooden spade, to prevent roasting. Drying time depended on the condition of the grain but often required considerably more than 24 hours processing before the miller judged it to be ready for milling. The customer, of course, was required to pay for drying 'his grain'.

A member of the 'Friends of Heage Windmill' made a model of the kiln, displayed in the Interpretation Centre so that details of its construction can be seen. (cf picture on previous page)

The Visitor and Interpretation Centres

The Visitor Centre is built on the footstep of the old kiln building, using as much of the old stone (local ironstone) as possible but with additional material provided from excavations on the site. Two toilets are included in the building with access for disabled persons.

The main body of the building houses a small shop where the visitor registers for a tour and can purchase light refreshments, drinks and ice cream etc. Various souvenirs of the windmill and Heage flour are on sale here and any profits made in the shop are used for the continued maintenance of the windmill.

In the adjacent undercroft to the mill is housed the Interpretation area, where there are 22 large display panels which tell the story of the windmill and her restoration. These are supported by an audio visual presentation and by the display of various mill artefacts.

Pat and Celia in the sales area of the Visitor Centre

A Simple Guide To How The Mill Operates

Dave Bent dressing the French burr runner stone

In the past wheat was brought to the mill in sacks (probably weighing 280 pounds [127 kg]) in the farmer's cart and unloaded. It is possible that the sacks were then stored in the basement until the miller was ready to mill the wheat. Presently we purchase sealed sacks of pre-dried organic wheat, ready for milling.

When there was sufficient wind, which in the old days could be day or night, the miller would start the mill. Initially a check is made of the millstones to ensure they rotate freely; if not the upper stones are raised using the tentering gear. (Nowadays we mill as required and at other times just allow the sails to idle round). Following this it is necessary to release the brake by pulling on the rope hanging from under the cap near the fantail stage. This raises the brake beam until it is caught and held by a 'swinging' catch. Another pull on the rope releases the catch, then the beam descends and again operates the brake.

At this time the miller has to decide how to set the shutters on the sails. For a light wind the shutters will be closed fully to allow the sail to catch the wind and as the wind becomes stronger the shutters will be opened further. Pulling on the chain from the striking lever closes the shutters. This moves the striking rod through the windshaft and moves

The shutters are opened.

Holly, a miller, operating the sack hoist

the spider which opens or closes the shutters. The position of the shutters is maintained by hanging a weight on the chain. This acts as an automatic safety release should the wind increase when the shutters are set for a light wind; the pressure of the wind on the shutters will force them open by raising the chain with the weight.

Sacks of wheat are raised to the bin floor using the sack hoist. The hoist chain is passed through the ring on the end of the chain to make a loop, which is then placed round the top of the sack. By pulling on the hoist rope, the hoist is engaged and the sack is raised through trapdoors on the next two floors.

John adding grain to the hopper

Listening to the bangs as the trapdoors fall tells the miller the position of the sack and thus he knows when to release the hoist rope. If the miller is lucky the chain will release from the sack and descend ready to hoist the next sack. Otherwise he will have to climb to the appropriate floor, release the sack and lower the chain to the ground floor. The sacks are then emptied into the storage bin and the milling is ready to start.

On the stone floor it is then necessary to determine the feed rate. Above the stones is the feed hopper which is filled with wheat from the storage bins above and a slide valve at its base allows wheat to run into the shoe (a wooden trough). The shoe is inclined to allow the wheat to slide down into the eye, or central hole, of the runner (upper) stone.

On the shaft driving the runner stone is a square section against which a string is fastened to a wooden spring mounted on the tun (the wooden cover for the stones). As the shaft rotates it jars the shoe, causing the wheat to gently slide down the shoe. Both the inclination of the shoe and the opening of the slide valve can be altered to control the flow of wheat into the eye of the stone.

Once the wheat is flowing between the stones, the gap between the stones is adjusted on the meal, or ground floor, by slowly turning the tentering handle, whilst at the same time monitoring the flour coming down the chute from the stones. Once this is of the correct fineness, the governor maintains the stones at the correct gap, provided the wind does not alter drastically.

As the level of the wheat in the feed hopper runs down a bell rings as a warning, but it is generally better to keep checking the level and refilling the feed hopper from the bin above. The meal produced at this stage is wholemeal flour but this can then be passed through the dresser in order to produce white flour.

Heage Windmill
STONE GROUND
MIDDLINGS
produced from organic grain
1.5 Kg

Heage Windmill
STONE GROUND
WHOLEMEAL FLOUR
produced from organic grain
1.5 Kg

Something about Flour

Flour is the result of milling (by whatever process) the grains of the wheat plant. In earlier times various types of flour for bread making were produced from rye, barley, oats and peas as well as from wheat. In some parts of the world some of these 'flours' are still made and used; the Germans make a considerable amount of rye bread.

Two obvious differences are found when examining flour; there are both white and brown flours available. White flour is made from the same wheat as brown flour; the difference is that the white flour has had some portion of the wheat removed during milling operations. It may also have had other things deliberately added at that time.

In commercial roller milling it is possible to produce a large variety of flours by altering the blends of the types of wheat used in the mill and also by extracting the flour at different points in the milling process but this is not possible in the traditional mill. Additionally each miller has differing names for his various flours, thus making a certain difficulty for the baker wishing to change supplier, as he will then have to experiment to find a suitable matching type.

A guide to some types of flour

Extraction rate*: This term is used by millers to indicate the amount of flour extracted from the wheat. 100% extraction produces wholemeal flour.*

White Flour

This results from the separation made during the milling process and sometimes the blend of different types of wheat. White flour typically has an extraction rate of 72%: i.e. 100 kg of wheat produces 72 kg of white flour, the remainder is bran and wheatgerm.

'Brown' Flours

Wholemeal - (sometimes called wholewheat) - is the flour produced when the whole of the wheatgrain, bran, endosperm and germ is milled and thus nothing is removed. It should, however, be noted that much commercial wholemeal flour is made by first making white flour (complete with all its additives) and then adding the bran and germ back into the product. Brown is a current term used to describe wheatmeal flour.

Hovis: This is a trade name (belonging to Rank Hovis McDougall) for a white flour that has had concentrated wheat germ added to it.

Granary: This is the proprietary name of a blend of wheatmeal, rye flour and pieces of malted wheat grain. It produces bread with a sweetish taste and slightly sticky texture.

Organic: Flour milled from wheat grown and processed naturally without the use of chemicals. There are official bodies who approve the use of the term 'organic' and whose seal may then appear on the bag of approved flour.

Heage Flours

The flour we produce at Heage is all made from organic wheat and we offer it in various forms:

Wholemeal - just as the meal comes off the stones

White flour - after sieving

Middlings, *Coarse Brown* and *Bran* - these being different grades of the residue from the separation of wholemeal when we produce white flour.

Flour on sale at Belper Farmers Market

Our flour is produced and packaged entirely at the mill and is 100% stone ground. It is only sold at the mill and at Farmers Markets, where the stalls are always staffed by Friends of Heage Windmill.

A Commentary On The Heritage Value Of The Mill

The importance of the mill has been recognised by the local authorities and statutory bodies by the listing as a building of great historic interest, Grade II*. The listing reads:

"CI8. Three storeys, circular coursed rubble tower mill.

Stone framed windows. Onion dome with six common sails, and remains of tail fan staging. Multiple sailed mills are distinctly uncommon. (Restored 1971-3)"

Note the errors: the existing sails were not 'common sails' but frames for 'patent sails' and the cap would normally be described as 'ogee'.

The listing is a very brief summary of the visual and historic value of the mill building. It is desirable to enlarge upon the points listed, and to note a number of other important original features, which render it unusual, in some cases unique, and make it a very interesting example of industrial history. These include:

　i) The tower is constructed from the local sandstone, which has mellowed into most attractive colours and texture. The stone was restored and the mill repointed in 2001/2. Stone mill towers are comparatively rare, and this one reflects the appropriate use of local material which is believed to have been dug from the quarry like depression to the west of the mill.

The substantial stone window and door casings are typical of the age and area, and make the whole a well preserved example of local 18th century vernacular industrial construction. Its relatively large diameter gives it a rather squat appearance, which is typical of the earlier tower mills in Derbyshire.

　ii) The cap is a large diameter ogee ('onion' shape), which appears to have been typical of the earlier Derbyshire tower mills, and is the only complete one remaining in the county. During an earlier restoration it was re-covered with aluminium sheets, which was expedient at the time to provide an economic

2001 Restoration: excavating stone from original quarry site.

weatherproof covering. The 2002 restoration has resulted in the whole cap being refurbished and recovered in traditional material.

iii) The use of six sails is very rare, the normal number of sails in Britain being four.

There are only two other six sailed mills extant (Waltham and Sibsey Trader, both in Lincolnshire, and both with significant detail differences to Heage), and only one mill in the whole of the British Isles with any greater number (Heckington, Lincolnshire, with eight sails).

There were formerly a few other six sailed mills, mainly in Lincolnshire, with just one other example in Derbyshire, nearby at Riddings. A second windmill at Riddings was also built, but the sails were never fitted, although a windshaft with six arm cross was installed. However, the Riddings Mills were of the tall, narrow brick Lincolnshire type and could not be called typical Derbyshire mills; all re-

'James' at Riddings, the only other six sailer in Derbyshire.

mains of them have now disappeared. Heage is the only complete stone-built tower mill in the British Isles retaining more than four sails and must therefore be considered an important example, both locally and nationally.

iv) The use of a six-arm cast iron cross on the windshaft is rare. It is necessary to enable six sails to be fitted to a mill, and again Waltham and Sibsey Trader are the only other extant examples in the country.

v) The arms of the cast iron cross at Heage are of a particularly robust form of construction. They are constructed in the form of a channel section and are unusually heavily ribbed at the back, with cast bosses for the sail shackles.

vi) The 'shot curb' is one of the few examples in Britain, and the only one in the region. It incorporates a roller race having a large number (24) of equally spaced cast iron rollers around the curb, fixed in cast iron yokes with wrought iron spacer bars, and free from both the curb of the tower and the cap.

It is guided by running in a channel section of the cast iron curb, but the underside of the cap circle that runs on the topside of the rollers is only a plain iron plate. The cap itself is kept correctly centred by means of horizontal truck, or steady, wheels which bear on the inside face of the curb. The cast iron curb edge is effectively lipped which performs the second important function of restraining the cap from being blown off by the wind.

The design details are perhaps a result of the reconstruction being undertaken by the Butterley Company, as they reflect fairly advanced engineering practice rather than normal windmill practice. There is however one common drawback to a shot curb resulting from the ensuing lack of frictional resistance which can be disadvantageous in a windmill as it can fail to provide sufficient damping to reduce unwanted buffeting in the wind. Fortunately this has not proved to be a problem during subsequent operation.

vii) The use of a double drive system for the fantail drive is unusual and again was probably introduced by the Butterley Company. The system may have the advantage of a smoother drive than a single pinion, and was perhaps introduced to counteract the 'buffeting' effect associated with a shot curb. The system is illustrated on page 10 in the drawing made in 1962.

viii) The wooden bevelled cogs on the brakewheel were at some stage removed and cast iron toothed rim plates substituted, to match the cast iron wallower that must also have been replaced at the same time. Although this is not an uncommon practice, it does provide an inter-

Rhydlyham double cogged great spur wheel.
cf text **x)** overleaf.

Cruck timber brake beam with pulley ropes

esting example of development in gearing.

ix) The cruck timber brake beam is most unusual. It is not easy to ascertain the benefit to be obtained from using this highly bent timber.

x) Of extreme interest is the great spur wheel. It is of timber clasp arm construction, and also was originally fitted with two rows of mortised wooden cogs, staggered by half a pitch (cf photo on p41). The object appears to have been to provide a smoother drive in comparison with the coarser pitch that would have been required for a single row of cogs. However, the increased complexity cannot have been justified as very few other examples of this technique are found; this is the only remaining timber example in a windmill. One practical disadvantage may have been the limiting effect on vertical travel when adjusting the stones or 'tentering' the mill.

The great spur wheel was, like the brakewheel, modified at some time by the fitting of cast iron toothed rim segments, but these were removed before 1970 and no evidence of their form or that of the matching stone nuts has been found. In the 2002 restoration work a single row of bolt-on cast iron cogs has been adopted, as was the case when the mill was last in commercial operation.

xi) The double fold entrance doors to the front and the rear of the mill are an interesting use of this design to provide more working space within the mill building, whilst having a large opening. They also have the function of allowing entry to the mill irrespective of the position of the sails.

xii) The fireplace on the ground floor with its brick lined flue buried in the wall approximately 5m above ground is an interesting feature. The flue cap on the outside of the mill is missing.

xiii) The basement provides an interesting use of space on the sloping site, though its original function is not now clear. It is known that at some point it was used as a stable and it is entered via an original stone flagged passage way which was buried before the restoration under 2 feet of debris. This area is now used as an interpretation centre, to provide visitors with information on the windmill.

The remainder of the machinery is conventional and some was brought from other mills during the 1970 restoration. It is all, however, appropriate for the type of mill.

Recognition Of The Windmill Restoration

The actual restoration of the windmill was carried out over a period of about two years (2000-2) by a team of dedicated contractors, ably supported by many willing, and often very cold and wet, volunteers. Throughout the work every effort was made to ensure that a very high standard of workmanship was maintained and that the traditional features of the windmill were maintained, and a number of awards were received, recognising the restoration.

The Heage Windmill Trust was particularly delighted to learn from the Mills Section of SPAB (Society for the Protection of Ancient Buildings) that the windmill had been awarded the '13th SPAB Windmill Plaque' in recognition of the high standards achieved, the hard work of all involved and the plans for the continued maintenance of the mill. The bronze plaque was presented to Gordon Hardy, Chairman of the Trust, by Mrs Mildred Cookson, chairman of the Mills Section on September 11th, 2004, and is displayed above the south door of the mill.

Presentation of SPAB Windmill plaque, September 2004
Alan Gifford, Mildred Cookson, Gordon Hardy, Cllr G Carlile

The Shore Family and Milling

Thomas Shore, born in 1877, was the last miller to work the mill until she ceased commercial operations in 1919 and he was an artist of some local repute. The Shore family however has a much longer pedigree. Sir John Shore of Derby (1616-1680) was a doctor of medicine and the main stream of the family appears to stem from him, with branches in many parts of the country.

The Shores married into various titled aristocratic lines and a John Shore, of Heage, married Hannah Elliott, in Duffield, in 1785. Their children were Isaac (b 1788), John (b 1801), and Hannah. Isaac (a clock maker 1851 census) married Mary Wainwright of Heage and they had three boys, Enoch (b 1813) and Thomas (b 1815), later of the Tower House 10, Malthouse Lane, Heage, (a **miller** and also grocer – information from Max Craven) and Isaac (b 1819), another **miller**. Thomas was a prolific writer for the *'Original Methodists' Record* newsletter, and died in April 1886. Pigot's Directory, in 1846, records that Isac and John Shore were **millers**.

The brothers appear to have commenced **milling** activities in about 1842 (tithe records) at the water and steam mills below the windmill, at the bottom of Dungely Hill, and to have bought Heage windmill in about 1850. It therefore became the only milling business we know of in the country which was powered by wind, water and steam.

Isaac had two sons, Enoch and Joseph Smith Shore (b 1844 & 1854) both of whom were **millers**. Isaac, and later, his son Joseph, lived for a time at Heage Hall and when he left there Joseph built a bungalow in Slack Lane, Nether Heage. He recorded the fact with his initials on one of the window lintels 'JSS 1925'. His son Thomas Isaac (b 1877) was a talented local artist and, as noted above, he was the last commercial **miller** at Heage windmill.

It is also interesting to note that a William Shore married into the family of the rich lead merchant, Peter Nightingale, of nearby Lea Hall. To preserve the Nightingale line he took that family name and his daughter was the famous Florence Nightingale, of nursing fame - so she really was a Shore too!

Note – The above represents the best present day appreciation of this family's milling involvement. Any additional information will be welcomed. **AFG 1/04/07**

Millers who worked at Heage Windmill

Source	Date	Name	Entry
Advertisement	1798	James Turton, Crich	'will let mill'
Advertisement	1802	Joseph Booth (or Rooth)	occupier
Advertisement	1805	R Ashley	occupier
Advertisement	1808	William Norman deceased	miller
Advertisement	1816	J Walters	'on the premises'
Advertisement	1816	Mr Whysall	'Mare Hay Nr. Ripley'
Parish Register	1820	William Simpson	miller
Parish Register	1820	Samuel Argile	miller
Parish Register	1823	Abraham Whysall	miller
Glover	1829	Joseph Morrell	miller - victualler (at 'Black Boy')
Parish Register	1830	Thomas Renshaw	miller
Pigot	1835	No miller listed	
Pigot	1842	No miller listed	
Tithe Award	1843	Samuel Hawkins	miller/occupier
Advertisement	1846	William Clark & Samuel Hawkins: roles not clear	
Pigot	1846	Isaac & John Shore	residents
Bagshawe	1846	William Clark	miller - victualler (at 'Black Boy')
Bagshawe	1846	Thomas, Isaac & John Shaw (Shore): millers	
Slater	1850	No miller listed	
White	1857	Clark & Hawkins	millers
White	1857	Edward Gell	managing corn miller
Harrison Harrod	1860	Isaac Shore & Co	millers
Harrison Harrod	1870	Shore, Messrs	millers
Kelly	1876	Isaac Shore & Co	millers
Kelly	1881	Isaac Shore & Co	millers & farmers
Kelly	1891	Joseph & Enoch Shore	millers
Bulmer	1895	Shore, Isaac & Co. (Enoch & Joseph Smith Shore) Over Heage	wind mill, millers & corn factors
Kelly	1895	Shore, Joseph & Enoch,	millers (steam, water & wind), & farmers.
Kelly	1900	Shore, Joseph & Enoch,	millers (steam, water & wind), & farmers & coal owners
Cook	1903	No miller listed	
Kelly	1908	Joseph & Enoch Shore	millers & farmers
Kelly	1912	Shore, Joseph & Enoch	farmer, Heage Hall
Family data	1919	Thomas Isaac Shore	miller at closure
Kelly	1922	No mention of Shore running a business or the windmill	

The names - Glover, Pigot, Bagshawe, Slater, White, Harrison Harrod, Kelly, Bulmer all refer to Derbyshire Trade Directories, published in the year shown.

Selected Data On Heage Windmill				
Building	Ft/ins	Metres	Other Information
Tower height to curb (415' 8" – 126.69m above sea level)	26' 3"	8.0	Stone
Cap interior height	13' 2"	3.0	Wooden
Total mill height	39' 5"	11.0	
Tower dia. (exterior)	22' 11"	7.0	
Curb dia. (exterior)	19' 4"	5.9	
Number of doors			2 (plus 1 to undercroft)
Number of windows			7
Cap and Sails			
Total weight with fittings			13.5 tonnes
Windshaft weight			1.5 tonnes approx.
Windshaft length	16' 11"	5.1	Cast iron
Windshaft max. dia.	9¾"	0.25	
Length of whips (sails)	30' 0"	9.0	
Width of sail bay	6' 0"	1.83	
Width of leading boards	9"	0.225	
Total area of sails	900 sq.ft.	90 sq.m.	
Fan tail dia.	11' 4"	3.45	
Machinery			
Brake Wheel dia.	8' 0"	2.44	Wooden
Brake Wheel width	11"	0.28	
Brake Wheel No. of teeth			100 cast iron
Wallower dia.	3' 4"	1.02	Cast iron
Wallower No. of teeth			45
Great Spur Wheel dia.	6' 0"	1.83	Wooden
Great Spur Wheel No. of teeth			84 cast iron
Upright Shaft length	17' 9"	5.41	Wooden
Upright Shaft dia.	18" av.	0.46	
Overall gear ratio (stones:sails)			Approx. 10:1
Stones			
Stone Nut overall dia.	18"	0.46	Cast iron core
Stone Nut No. of cogs			20 apple wood
Millstones dia.	4' 6"	1.37	French & Derbyshire
Millstones weight			1 tonne approx.
Operational Data			
Sail r.p.m.			8 - 10 (best operation)
Stone speed r.p.m.			Up to 120 approx.
Flour milled per hour			100kg max.

The Beaufort Scale and Windmills

The Beaufort scale was introduced to the British Navy in 1805 by Admiral Sir Francis Beaufort who wanted to devise a method for ships to report wind conditions in the ship's log. He used the ship's performance in different winds as his measure, so he was actually recording the force of the wind and not its speed. The scale has since been modified to suit land use and has also been updated at various times. The reaction of a windmill at various scales is indicated below:-

Beaufort Scale

	Description	m.p.h.	m/sec	Pressure lbs/sq ft	English Windmill :-
2	Gentle wind	5	2.24	0.125	Unlikely to start
3	Breeze	8	3.58	0.33	Just about starts
		10	4.77	0.5	Runs slowly
		12	5.36		Runs well/mills
4	Good wind	13	5.81		
		15	6.71	1.25	Runs steadily/mills
5	Strong wind	18	8.05		
		20	8.94	2.0	Gives best service
		23	10.28		
6	Very strong wind	25	11.18	3.125	Maximum safe use
7	Fresh gale	27	12.07		Sails furled
8	Gale	30	13.41	4.5	Battens down
9	Heavy gale	40	17.89	8.0	Miller prays!

(Adapted from 'Power from the Wind',
Rev. Dr R L Hills 1996, CUP)

The Mill On The Hill At Heage

This painting, by Thomas Isaac Shore, the last miller, demonstrates a naïve, old fashioned quality which is ably complemented by this evocative poem by Douglas Gifford.

This windmill was built with sails only four
But a hundred years later its power was poor.
So when damage occurred they learned a few tricks
And the number of sails just went up to six.
The fantail was fitted, turns sails the right way
'Cuz the wind don't blow the same way each day.
It's not just made of wood like a cheap post mill
It really is a wonderful mill.

Under the cap at the top you will see
Wonderful things to delight you and me.
There's old iron gears still working well
The grease of their bearings gives out a sweet smell.
There's a rack and a track to turn the cap
There's also a brake to prevent the mishap.
Look through the window out at the hill,
See beautiful views from this wonderful mill.

Then two floors down and here grinds the grain
Between stones, driven, cut and run just the same.
Down the chutes runs the freshly ground flour,
The millstones are driven by strong windy power.

Between each floor there's a very steep stair
So as you climb take very great care.
Look at the walls, the quaint fire and sill
You are really in a wonderful mill.

The history's been told and you will soon go
But remember your visit, for now you will know
At Heage early millers were the brothers Shore,
When they ran the mill their word was law.
When lightning struck, the sails were stilled,
And the grain in the carts could not be milled.
In nineteen nineteen no more could she mill,
The kiss of death to this wonderful mill.

Fifty years on, though there was no need,
For the mill to be used to grind the corn seed,
A new cap was fitted and sails were replaced.
It helped save the stones but t'was done in haste.
Now you can see after thirty more years
With lottery money and a whole lot of tears.
The mill was restored by great effort of will
The kiss of life to this wonderful mill.

Douglas Gifford. 25 April 2002
(deceased May 2007)